CELEBRATING THE FAMILY NAME OF ZHAO

Celebrating the Family Name of Zhao

Walter the Educator

Silent King Books
a WhichHead Entertainment Imprint

Copyright © 2024 by Walter the Educator

All rights reserved. No part of this book may be reproduced in any manner whatsoever without written permission except in the case of brief quotations embodied in critical articles and reviews.

First Printing, 2024

Disclaimer

This book is a literary work; the story is not about specific persons, locations, situations, and/or circumstances unless mentioned in a historical context. Any resemblance to real persons, locations, situations, and/or circumstances is coincidental. This book is for entertainment and informational purposes only. The author and publisher offer this information without warranties expressed or implied. No matter the grounds, neither the author nor the publisher will be accountable for any losses, injuries, or other damages caused by the reader's use of this book. The use of this book acknowledges an understanding and acceptance of this disclaimer.

Celebrating the Family Name of Zhao is a memory book that belongs to the Celebrating Family Name Book Series by Walter the Educator. Collect them all and more books at WaltertheEducator.com

USE THE EXTRA SPACE TO DOCUMENT YOUR FAMILY MEMORIES THROUGHOUT THE YEARS

ZHAO

Zhao, a name of ancient lore,

Whose roots run deep in history's core.

From distant plains to mountains high,

Its legacy spreads beneath the sky.

With banners raised and hearts so pure,

The Zhao name stands, strong and sure.

A lineage bold, a tale profound,

In every corner, its echoes resound.

Through dynasties of silk and stone,

The Zhao name carved a path alone.

In fields of wisdom, art, and might,

It flourished like the morning light.

The phoenix rises, a symbol proud,

The Zhao name spoken clear and loud.

A flame of honor, a steady guide,

With Zhao, tradition and truth abide.

Through trials fierce, in peace or war,

The Zhao name grows, forevermore.

Its roots in soil both rich and vast,

A bridge connecting present and past.

Like rivers winding to the sea,

The Zhao family moves with harmony.

With every turn, a lesson shared,

A legacy built on love and care.

The ink of scholars, the sword of knights,

The Zhao name shines in all its rights.

A name that holds the strength of time,

Its rhythm echoes in every rhyme.

In every heart, a dream takes flight,

Inspired by Zhao's enduring light.

A heritage shaped by courage and skill,

A steadfast force, a mighty will.

The Zhao name dances with the breeze,

Whispered in forests, sung by seas.

A symphony played through generations,

A testament to its bold foundations.

So here's to Zhao, a name revered,

A family cherished, deeply endeared.

Through time it stands, through all it grows,

A story of triumph, the Zhao name shows.

ABOUT THE CREATOR

Walter the Educator is one of the pseudonyms for Walter Anderson. Formally educated in Chemistry, Business, and Education, he is an educator, an author, a diverse entrepreneur, and he is the son of a disabled war veteran. "Walter the Educator" shares his time between educating and creating. He holds interests and owns several creative projects that entertain, enlighten, enhance, and educate, hoping to inspire and motivate you. Follow, find new works, and stay up to date with Walter the Educator™

at WaltertheEducator.com

www.ingramcontent.com/pod-product-compliance
Lightning Source LLC
LaVergne TN
LVHW052009060526
838201LV00059B/3934